Nightfire

GAIL MAZUR

Nightfire

DAVID R. GODINE · BOSTON

10/1978
Gift: Abe,

David R. Godine, Publisher
Boston, Massachusetts

★

Copyright © 1978
by Gail Mazur
LCC 77–94476
ISBN 0–87923–242–0
Printed in the United States of America

Acknowledgments: Magazines and anthologies in which some of these poems previously appeared are: *Arion's Dolphin*; *The Blacksmith Anthologies 1 & 2*; *Dark Horse*; *Green House*; *Io Anthology: Baseball I Gave You All the Best Years of My Life*; *The Nantucket Review*; *Ploughshares*; *The Real Paper*; *SUN*; *Zeugma*. The author wishes to express gratitude to the National Endowment for the Arts for a Creative Writing Fellowship which aided in the completion of this book.

A Godine Poetry Chapbook
Third Series

Contents

Seeing Bats in Cambridge

she says they make her think of Bela Lugosi
and laughs
but really she's remembering her father
wildly swinging a broom in her bedroom
herself under blankets hiding her long hair
from the blind claws

that was at the Cape house
where a different one of the cats
would go wild each summer
and she'd spot them in the woods
gleaming, sprinting like ocelots

she'd crawl deep into sumac and catbriar
calling the cat's name
invisible snakes rustled in the vines

bats make her think swamp alligators
and quicksand nights
watching them black in the sky
she feels cornered again,
cringing under covers, rabid
believing their high-pitched calls

Poison Ivy

those summers swollen and wildly itching
until she was nearly a woman
it followed her everywhere
at the farm
where manure steamed by the barn
and Kentucky Wonders waited to be picked

she lay oozing and alone in a dark room
hoping she was Rima about to rise
from green mansions

even in January her skin
would remember the itch
the hot sting of a shower
or an absent minded scratching
bringing it speckling back

until her seasons changed
and June stopped meaning wild alarm to her
and the others after a while
stopped saying
"she has only to look at it"
and so forth

as if she were a witch
casting spells
only on herself

so the infection
when it would still come
was mild and the sensation bearable
accustomed as she had become to self-restraint
and the shutting down of desire

still who can forget
an itch like that
and she yearning to ripen
learned such a careful dread
that this September
walking the Cape road
and seeing ivy choke the swelling grapes
she shivers and is cold

Nightfire

This must be the fire,
the one that parents lie awake for,
planning rescue,
planning escape.

My father smells it
and gets us out of bed.
He herds us together
and climbs on the back window ledge,
calling the neighbors for help.

We huddle at the front,
at the window of my brother's room.
We must look like the Royal Family
without the King,
standing together at the window
after a wedding,
waving for help.

The Barker boys,
who live next door,
come quickly with a ladder.
Paul, the tallest, clambers up
to take my little sister down,
then comes back for me.

I cling to the window frame,
unwilling to let go.
Don't be afraid, he tells me,
professional as a fireman,
the one who holds you in his arms
but cannot quite put out the fear.

He carries me down
to the yard but gives me to his brother.
Mother is next, then brother Jon,
who, nearly at the bottom, looks up
to see my father climbing on.

I tremble on the grass,
hunched with a bunch of nosy neighbors,
watching Daddy, a blanket wrapped
around his waist, standing at the top,
the ladder cracking, swaying toward us.
The terrible drop.

The crowd is pleased.
It didn't get out of bed for nothing.
It's had a fire and an injured man.
No false alarm.

My father goes to the hospital.
We are taken in next door, smelly,
without a thing to wear.
The Barker boys go off to work,
to war, to marriage,
I am in love with Paul for years.

Soon, the woman who helps
around the house arrives
to scrub for months, throw out
the smoky clothes we'll never wear
again. New windows are installed,
the walls are papered, the kitchen,
where the Frigidaire exploded,
is redone. My father recovers.

But nights,
when my homework is finished,
I lie awake in bed,
my room crisp and clean,
and listen for the fire
like a lover's whisper,
whistling up the stairs.

Then I Had Two Friends,

Juno and a 15¢ notebook
whom I addressed in the manner,
Dear Diary.
Volumes followed, desolation packed,
full of resolutions.

Juno, black except in the sun
when she shone mahogany,
trusted me enough
to have one litter of kittens
under my sheets while I slept
and forgave my screams
when I woke with wet feet.

She slept at my shoulder,
sucking the pajama sleeve,
kneading her dream of infancy.
Licked my hands and face
with sandpaper tongue.
So beautiful, to look at her
eased the knots that were growing.

Her tail had been bitten off at birth
by a too-fervid mother,
her own litters I forbade my father
to drown as he had drowned others,
we children loathing him
in our house on the river.

Born when I was 8, she disappeared
when I was 23 and pregnant
with my second child.
Secretly departed my parents' house,
and though my father walked the neighborhood
for nights, calling,
never reappeared.

Gone as neatly
as she had washed her paws,
choosing her end alone.

The cat didn't need as I needed,
and the cats since,
and as I write in this notebook,
those children downstairs,
born in the end of her years,
impatient now to leave.

Sundays

for my grandfather

Mother cooked in the afternoon
while I, who had never known you
without your swollen knuckles,
your tortured knees and elbows,
who took your affliction for granted,
sat in the den with you, and listened.

Snug on the couch, I heard the myths
you reinvented every week, your war
at San Juan Hill, your pal who spat
rivers, your wicked stepmother,
her mouth malicious as sin,
the schoolmaster who caned young boys,
the bullies you whipped, outwitted
like a Jewish Huck Finn.

My state-of-Maine grandfather,
when you sang "The Bowery" in a beery voice,
I thought you'd really been a bum
and wondered who had saved you.

With fingers swollen like darning eggs,
you brushed the crumbs of Sunday dinner
from your hand-me-down pinstripe suit.
Your world shrank to the rooms
you lived in, your weekly trips to us.

I outgrew you.
I knew you waited half the day
before you'd call to say hello,
dialling with the stub of a pencil.
I'd answer, impatient as a duchess,
seething with adolescence.
I couldn't talk to you or listen.
I gave you the "bum's rush", you'd say.

Doc, my bantam-cock grandfather,
rough as the Bowery, salty as Maine,
I was restless, mole-blind in the den,
our Sunday cage, Mother cooking
her grief away, whole biographies
bubbling on the kitchen stove.

Waiting

1.

At first, helpless at the news,
still playing house,
he buys flowers for their room,
anemones. Whatever is growing
between them, they welcome it,
eager for new memories.

2.

The turnpike dream:
driving on Rte. 3,
she is responsible
for a mosquito's life.
It flies against the windshield,
she slams the brakes,
too late.

3.

The landlord,
painting their tenement himself,
takes sick
with only the back wall finished.
He paints his name
BEN ISRAEL
across the front.
Letters dripping,
he goes indoors to die.

4.

She dreams she carries
something alive in a shoebox.
A small clock for heartbeat
keeps it company.
At the supermarket,
she places it on the shelf
but later with the muzak droning
she can't remember which aisle:
paper products
soups and cereals
baked goods?
Either it's lost
or someone is taking it home.

5.

In summer heat,
day trips to the state park.
Wading in the shadow
of the Sleeping Giant,
her body plays an old joke:
looking straight down,
she can't see her toes.

6.

A cat adopts them.
They name it Kitty
and take it everywhere.
Walking on the country road,
Kitty goes into convulsions.
That night, sleepless,

they try to conjure the future.
Brain-damaged Kitty finally runs away.

7.

She likes the idea of growing
an avocado, but the toothpicks
in the seed seem cruel.
In a jelly glass
it waits like an egg,
the small slit promising,
life coiling from inside,
the fragile stem and first leaf.

8.

The new doctor asks what family diseases.
Diabetes, gout, arthritis,
and during her engagement
she always had diarrhea.
Fine. He's benign, strange to her.
All she can say on the labor table,
the December blizzard raging outside,
scopalamine making her silly,
is *Florida, Florida.*

9.

Riding out on the table,
the cruel instructions receding,
her son shimmers beside her.
She thinks she'll always remember
haze, the gold film,
the radiant beginning.

Country House: November

Another break-in.
We're getting used to it.
Shattered windows,
drawers lolling out of chests
like imbecile tongues, beer cans

on the empty bed.
There's nothing we can do.
The country policeman drives in.
A mockery of detective work:
"Any fingerprints? These your gloves?"

No clues.
My father and I, alone together
for the first time in years,
search the dark house
for nails to fix the doors

to their frames.
We haul dead pines childishly
to camouflage the road.
Will they ever let us alone?
Hooligans, breaking the dead

quiet of the years.
The old house, empty so long,
its faded shutters hanging askew
like an aging fighter's ears,
wants to be left in peace. Or wants

to be filled with all of us
again. Father, how foolish we are
pretending the branches will protect
us, planning parties and dances.
Profusions again in the garden! Berries,

melons, beans!
Barricading, happy, singing
in the November cold, alone together
for the first time in years, we secretly
thank the burglars for what they stole.

Borges and I

My son tries to analyze this story:

The man, Borges, receives a letter from a friend.
"I have translated a poem by so-and-so,
who just died."

Borges decides to write the poet's biography.
His investigation yields this fact:
the poet was in the war of 1906
but was a coward.

Time passes.

The biographer Borges returns to interview his friend,
who says he never heard of the poet
and never translated the poem.
But another old soldier says the fellow was a hero
and *died* in the 1906 war.

The past cannot be changed but the memory can change
and the results of the past.
Life is a dream.
There is more than one reality.
Conflicting facts do co-exist.

The concepts *dream reality fact* have no meaning

Danny goes into the room to start writing his paper.
I sit at my desk
writing about his paper.
Where is Borges?
Argentina is declared in a state of siege.
Where is Danny?

I Dream of Responsibility

The Viennese doctor seems pleased to see me. "Were you able to help that young man," she asks, "Mark Dubke?"

This is a sudden reminder: I'm not only a teacher but a doctor as well, member of the Niagara Analytic Association.

And I've neglected my patients. Mark Dubke. Mark Dubke. *Who is he?* A boy whose eyes swim with confusion, who breathes intellectual hesitation.

My patients! I've forgotten them! Every appointment broken. Dubke, alone in his futile room, writing his last notes to his mother and doctor.

We fail him.

And my students, waiting in the seminar room while I make excuses to the Viennese woman. I try to get to the class but the custodian is washing down the stairs.

I climb the fire escape, sway over pavement and land in the art studio. The students are smearing the walls with oils. No door to this room.

I can hear my poor class disintegrating across the hall, the sound of ice breaking up on the spring river.

Mark Dubke, my student, begins to drown.

Ann-Olive's Voice

for Käthe

Ann-Olive travels about with a little voice.
The Voice stays around her ear, and, of course,
usually sounds like Ann-Olive's mother.
It plays the eardrum day and night,
saying commonplace things like
"You look ugly today" and
"They don't like you" and "Dumbo,
shut up" and calling Ann-Olive Clumsy.

Sometimes the Voice appears to take a vacation.
Conversation occurs.
Ann-O tells brilliant jokes,
her charm is acknowledged.
She briefly considers tennis and skiing.
Passage might be booked to Paris.
Then the Voice returns and there's too much baggage.
All trips are off.

When Ann-Olive sits down to write,
the Voice gives its Big Performance.
It dances in her ear like static,
singing staccato, "Stupid that stinks!"
and like a syncopated Sinatra,
"Don't you know little fool you
never can win use your mentality
wake up to reality" etc etc

Lunch

Utensils clang around her fingers. You've
twisted your white paper napkin until it's half
string. It looks like an albino mouse you're
swinging by the tail.

When she points this out to you, you throw
it under the table.

Poor mouse, its feelings injured, twitches
for a minute at her feet. Lies still, pretending
to be a napkin.

Napkin waits, deciding on a course of action,
knowing blondes are afraid of mice and of albinos.
They've just escaped being albinos themselves and
hate to be reminded of the pallid, mousey side of
things.

On the table, fork and knife play a nasty
duet. You feel like suggesting a duel. Her first
choice of weapons: *words*. You choose paper, which
makes her laugh triumphant, knowing she'll tromp
all over you.

But as she opens her mouth to speak, you
reach under the table for the napkin, careful to
grab it by the tail end. So it won't be you that
it bites.

The Sleeping Giantess
for Elsa Dorfman

You're a fly on the wall
you're in the bedroom
of the Sleeping Giantess
her bed is like the rolling hills
of Connecticut
the room is a state park
she herself is a national monument
someone else has crept in
he's waded through everything
who is it? he's kissing her
the Kiss of Life
the drapes ripple
around the body of the Great Slumberess
she's beginning to waken
her eyes open hazel and dreamy
green flecked as summer pond
her hands grope in the wilderness
for whatever it was she was doing
before she fell asleep
there's nothing there but empty spaces
she wasn't doing anything
before she fell into the Nap of the Century
her lover swoons back entranced
by the mounds moving beneath the green quilt
soft and round as Beverly Hills
the giantess rises
feels for her slippers
putting one enormous foot down
on the wooden floor

SOMETHING'S WRONG
she doesn't know what she's doing
she's crushed the man who
came to kiss her awake
squashed him out like a bad joke
with two of her toes
You watch with your tiny eye
the pulp spreading on the floor
proof that during her comatose years
someone was devoted devoted to her

All the Men in My Family Were Dentists

my father was a dentist.
I am a dental hygienist,
this work is my destiny.
Patients know they must come to me
before Doctor will see them.

I clean and polish their teeth,
I teach them to brush correctly,
to eat the proper foods.

I myself have never had so much
as a chocolate cherry.
Sometimes at the supermarket,
I see patients choosing cookies.
When they see me, they bounce
from the bakery counter
as if I had caught them stealing.

All day, in my office,
I work on their mouths,
Doctor in the next room
filling holes,
cheerful as Dentyne.
They like him,
the nervy women, the men
with their rotting teeth.

They send photographs of themselves
at Christmas, whole families
with grateful fluoride smiles,
To Doctor.

At night, I dream about them,
they come to me with garbage
caked under their gums.
I see myself scraping, scraping
at the pink flesh
with my pointed tools.
Making them bleed to be clean again.

I'd like to be the dentist,
I think.
When I ride on the subway at six,
hanging on the strap
I have to look down
at the yellow yawns,

those foul mouths
scream at me underground
and my hands are itching
to extract, extract.

Moving to Mars

You'll miss sex, you expect that.
But it won't make a wreck of you.
You know this is no honeymoon.
Your bags aren't packed with
tuxedos and new cumberbunds.

You're taking the minimum, you
tell me, packed into tubes like
free samples hanging on a back
doorknob—disposable razors,
anti-depressants, meals in a pill.

Where's the thrill in this move?
This isn't a film, you know,
the Red Desert, you'll be alone
out there in freezing non-weather,
pebbles and dust as far
as the eye can see.

There's no conversation,
no kissing or malicious gossip,
no tongues, in fact,
only the one you'll bring,
and that worn out
from flapping at me.

It's not everyone's Xanadu
but you choose it, waving goodby
from your intragalactic rocket,
my Polaroid exploding,
trying to fix your image,

you leaving me here
with burnt flashbulbs
and a feeling I'll forget.

The Adirondacks

My God it was raining and everything
between us had gone wrong.
Not that we didn't love each other—
we didn't—but even the basic mechanics.
I was so tired of peeing, et cetera,
in a tin pail and carrying the pail
out in the rain to empty it, carrying
in wet green logs. The supply of food,
even our staples, running out.
And speaking of staples, I couldn't
write anymore, no paper, no paper
clips, the last pencil past being
even a stub. You brooded in a tent
of blankets, not caring that everything
between us had gone wrong, not even
knowing we didn't love each other—
we didn't—I went out to empty
the tin pail, shivering and wet
as the first fish with feet that crawled
out of the ocean onto the beach—
I wondered if that was in Florida.
I was running out on you and slipped
on the wet step—who loaned us this cabin?
Some friend of yours who always hoped
we'd fall apart. I lay on the rocky
ground, I think my legs were broken,
staring at the Constellations, I only
recognized Orion and the Dippers and
Cassiopeia and no question about it,
I knew I was lost.

Enemies

Love, I enter your room like
a detective. When we touch I'm
searching your body for clues.

In truth, we're both spies, working
for hostile countries. Perverse as
adolescents, we fall in

love with the enemy: each
other. So easy to sabotage
a cause. Our superiors

can approve these seductions.
We've outsmarted them. We fly to
Barbados. My mission is

to recruit you. You've used a
similar excuse. Mornings we
tour the tropical gardens,

make love in our bungalow.
Hummingbirds whir iridescence
through the branches around us.

Our romance aches like a movie.
It can't last and we know it.
When the end comes, we try to

denounce each other, but you're
dragged off for interrogation,
your captors acting like colleagues.

All I know is we're saying
Good-bye. I watch your plane dissolve,
thinking, this is It, knowing

I've got to blunder out of
here, out of this spy story, though
my eyes sting in the real glare.

Living Alone: Cape Cod

walking the property line
edge of water scrub pines
the pebbly road Indian graves
savaged by catbriar
blueberry carpet gone sterile
in the shade poison ivy
red and angry lying
on the grassy knoll
at the lake watching jets
maneuvering in mock attack
thinking *what if bombs were falling*
would I creep for cover?
doubting it not caring at all

I'm moving more slowly
sleep in the morning groggy
all day awake at night only
moving my lips to eat to call the cat
at night the house empty hollow
woods dark as the past around me
ghosts in the bedrooms
the telephone rings:
Did I wake you?
mouth thick clumsy:
no – yes – no

Street Drawings, Sunday Morning

A chalk cat on the asphalt
mouths: THEY'RE EATING ME
into a gray balloon.
The blue dinosaur,
dissected by tire tracks,
pursues its powdery attack,
its jaws open, jagged, for cat
and elongated cockeyed girl.

She squeals EEK! HELP! in a bubble,
her ballet shoes and vermillion knees
disintegrating.

No rain is coming
to wash away the pastel menace
or the scribbled cries to the passerby.
The children who drew this scene
are in a backyard pool, splashing,
or still in bed,
thrashing out the last morning dream.

I read their tableau like a lesson,
as an archaeologist reads shards,
dusty clues preserved in the July drought,
and mammoths
are moving in the empty street.

Ossabaw Island

At the center, sunlight in a green clearing.
We settled in it, grateful as immigrants,
took off our shirts and leaned
against the liveoaks. Shadows of vines
hung noiseless as the idea of snakes,
copperheads and rattlers
shifting in January sleep.

Cows glared red-eyed from the deep wood.
The black feral pigs galumphing away
from us could have been our children,
the way you smiled as if
they were toddlers playing
In the palmettos. To me,
they looked like wild boar
thundering toward their victims.

We were so far from our house,
its books and noise, the rhythm
and blues on the stereo
our son and daughter dance to—
and then, lying on the warm earth,
the sad past of the South beneath us,
and above in the metaphor
of Spanish moss—

I wanted the children there,
to show them things:
shells, turds, small wild animals,
traces of rice plantations
and Indian kitchen midden,
the layers of this life.

Last Leaves

1.

Stomach pains. Early frost
blights the red dahlias
and the last petunias, purple
on my neighbor's stone wall.
Walking as fast as possible
to Harvard Square, but
still a sixteen-minute mile.
Thinking about my roommate,
Lynn, talking at dawn
over coffee and cigarettes.
That first fall, we talked
philosophy and sex.
Lynn, dead last year
of cancer. Thirty-six.

2.

Lynn, the only skinny one
of us. That first October,
we all took a rowboat on Paradise
Pond, and dry sandwiches
from the dormitory cooks.
The first time I'd felt close
to women. Lying on the grassy
bank, we watched maple leaves
drift to the water, milkweed
waiting to burst. We were happy,
having such friends, each other,

Lynn's thin fingers always held
a Winston, or pencils. The plunk
of oars that day, our picnic
giddy laughter, and not thinking
how distant we would be, or
had been. Place held us together,
a whole sweet afternoon of it.

3.

My daughter, home sick from school,
never knew those girls, except
in photographs, or the dormitory
nights we whispered everything
and then repeated everything.
We had no plans beyond week-ends,
ignored the Hungarian revolt.
My friends all drank too much,
I tried to learn, and couldn't,
despised them, held their heads,
Saturday after Saturday. Lynn,
it's not sentimental revision
to say: you were the nicest
of us. Simply that. Today,
I read your mother's letter,
still full of anger a year later
at how you suffered,
your three motherless boys.

4.

Driving the Mass Turnpike,
sign of the Pilgrim.
Layers of trees, turning in layers:
the old gold, red, dazzling grays.
At Howard Johnson's, English muffins
and a little pack of marmalade,
my son silent with his orange juice.
Filling the new Dodge with unleaded
and driving Danny to Middletown,
remembering the joke the children
loved from *Mad*: a whole cartoon family
chanting: JOHNSON'S HOWARD! JOHNSON'S
HOWARD! Whatever the joke is now,
they don't tell me.

5.

Eating alone in a Middletown restaurant,
I make a new rule for Connecticut:
leave *something* on the plate.
But I order apple pie and ice cream
and leave a tiny bite of apple:
always the letter of the law!
Still, the least resolution
is reason for rejoicing this fall,
feeling creaky,
driving my boy to college.

The Blackbirds Are Back in Kentucky

Their dark music menaces the towns
like the radio in the next room
that tells me about them
and then continues its loud jazz,
discordant as love cries.

They blacken the sky like an old plague,
and the townspeople have no prayers
to fight them with, have forgotten
the idea of an angry god.
They can only resort to poisons,
deadly and inadequate.

In the fall, you and I accept
New England's greying sky,
its wet yellow leaves.
There are many things we can't control,
even knowing of them in advance
and being intelligent.

Those troubles can't be planned for,
they swarm around us, swoop
with the arbitrariness of grand design.
Fatal accidents. Cancers. Divorcing.
Even witchcraft provides no shield.

We have nothing to do but wait
for the darkening, falling
in and out of love inevitably
as seasons and migrations,
your stubborn wings warm over me.

Nature disrupts this plot,
brings on the shadows
indestructible as a million blackbirds
insistent on settling
in the place they choose for themselves.

for Michael

Winter

Cambridge, 1976

Driving home from the movies,
I point at the skaters,
telling my children the current
makes the Charles unsafe.
Near the bridge, we can see
dark water swirling.

"People have drowned here,"
I tell them, "weighted down
with sweaters and skates.
They were too daring."

I'm full of warnings,
knowing how little time is left
for advice, knowing
this telling does no good.
I've lost subtlety.
My maxims, heavy and motherly,
bounce back at me in the cold air,

in my daughter's glare,
her life already taken care of.
Better, she's sure, than mine,
my stupid life.

I know I can't run ahead of her,
erecting signs that say DANGER
or THIN ICE. She thinks disaster
happens to strangers, actors
who'll reappear in a film
next year, in a different plot.

Neither can I follow behind.
I'm really no one's savior,
least of all my own, watching
the drama at the cold edge
of water, weighted with knowledge
and still waiting for rescue.

Baseball

for John Limon

The game of baseball is not a metaphor
and I know it's not really life.
The chalky green diamond, the lovely
dusty brown lanes I see from airplanes
multiplying around the cities
are only neat playing fields.
Their structure is not the frame
of history carved out of forest,
that is not what I see on my ascent.

And down in the stadium,
the veteran catcher guiding the young
pitcher through the innings, the line
of concentration between them,
that delicate filament is not
like the way you are helping me,
only it reminds me when I strain
for analogies, the way a rookie strains
for perfection, and the veteran,
in his wisdom, seems to promise it,
it glows from his upheld glove,

and the man in front of me
in the grandstand, drinking banana
daiquiris from a thermos,
continuing through a whole dinner
to the aromatic cigar even as our team

is shut out, nearly hitless, he is
not like the farmer that Auden speaks
of in Breughel's Icarus,
or the four inevitable woman-hating
drunkards, yelling, hugging
each other and moving up and down
continuously for more beer

and the young wife trying to understand
what a full count could be
to please her husband happy in
his old dreams, or the little boy
in the Yankees cap already nodding
off to sleep against his father,
program and popcorn memories
sliding into the future,
and the old woman from Lincoln, Maine,
screaming at the Yankee slugger
with wounded knees to break his leg

this is not a microcosm,
not even a slice of life

and the terrible slumps,
when the greatest hitter mysteriously
goes hitless for weeks, or
the pitcher's stuff is all junk
who threw like a magician all last month,
or the days when our guys look
like Sennett cops, slipping, bumping
each other, then suddenly, the play

that wasn't humanly possible, the Kid
we know isn't ready for the big leagues,
leaps into the air to catch a ball
that should have gone downtown,
and coming off the field is hugged
and bottom-slapped by the sudden
sorcerers, the winning team

the question of what makes a man
slump when his form, his eye,
his power aren't to blame, this isn't
like the bad luck that hounds us,
and his frustration in the games
not like our deep rage
for disappointing ourselves

the ball park is an artifact,
manicured, safe, "scene in an Easter egg",
and the order of the ball game,
the firm structure with the mystery
of accidents always contained,
not the wild field we wander in,
where I'm trying to recite the rules,
to repeat the statistics of the game,
and the wind keeps carrying my words away

PRI

DEMCO